D1321336

— THE GOURMET KITCHEN —

SUN-DRIED TOMATOES

WRITTEN BY ORLA BRODERICK
ILLUSTRATED BY SHARON SMITH

THE
APPLE
PRESS

A QUARTO BOOK

Published by The Apple Press
6 Blundell Street
London N7 9BH

ISBN 1-85076-553-7

This book was designed and produced by
Quarto Publishing plc.
The Old Brewery, 6 Blundell Street
London N7 9BH

Editors: Kate Kirby, Laura Washburn, Susan Ward
Art Editor: Mark Stevens
Designer: Julie Francis
Art Director: Moira Clinch
Editorial Director: Sophie Collins

Typeset in Great Britain by Central Southern Typesetters, Eastbourne, UK
Manufactured in Singapore by Eray Scan Pte. Ltd.
Printed in China by Leefung-Asco Printers Ltd.

Contents

INTRODUCTION

*F*or centuries, ripe Roma tomatoes have been dried in the hot Southern Italian sun. Explorers first brought the yellow tomato, named *pomodoro,* or golden apple, back to Europe in the sixteenth century. However, it was not until two Jesuits returned from Mexico with the seeds of a red variety that the tomato became an intrinsic part of Italian cooking.

Since their introduction, tomatoes have thrived in the Mediterranean summer sunshine; however, they need to be preserved for winter use. The Italians cultivate small, firm tomatoes, that grow in clusters, solely for this purpose. They are harvested in July and August, then hung in the sun until all the moisture has evaporated, leaving tomatoes that are leathery in texture and almost mahogany in colour. About seventeen pounds of fresh tomatoes produce one pound of dried.

Buying Sun-Dried Tomatoes

Introduced to the United States in 1980, and slightly later in Britain, sun-dried tomatoes are now part of the culinary scene. Sold in packages, as granules or paste, or packed in oil, sun-dried tomatoes are available from both American and Italian producers. You'll find sun-dried tomatoes in supermarkets, speciality food stores, gourmet cookware shops and Italian delicatessens.

Packaged dried tomatoes are less expensive and take up less storage space than those packed in oil, but they need to be re-constituted before using. Granules are sold in jars and may be sprinkled directly onto prepared dishes like a seasoning. The paste is sold in jars and tubes – a great convenience when you need only 1 or 2 tablespoons. Sun-dried tomatoes packed in oil are ready to use. However, it is less expensive and more re-warding to preserve your own.

Drying Tomatoes

If you live in a hot, dry climate, you might want to try drying tomatoes in the sun – the oldest form of food preservation. Ideally, you will need several consecutive days with temperatures above 29°C/85°F and relatively low humidity. Otherwise, you can dry them in an oven or a food dehydrator. How long this actually takes can vary drastically, depending on the variety of the tomatoes or even the rainfall during the growing season.

Preparing, Testing, and Storing Always choose firm ripe Roma tomatoes – beefsteak, cherry, and other varieties are too watery. Before drying, dip the tomatoes in boiling water, then ice water; dry, core, and halve them lengthways. Sprinkling with salt is a matter of personal preference. For a doubly delicious treat, use home-grown tomatoes.

To test for doneness after drying, cool a tomato, then taste; it should be chewy, even slightly leathery, with a concentrated sweet tomato flavour. Cool completely.

For sun-dried tomatoes, loosely pack in plastic bags or plastic or glass jars, and store at room temperature for 5–7 days, shaking occasionally to prevent sticking. This 'mellowing' allows any remaining moisture to be evenly

6

absorbed. For all dried tomatoes, freeze for 48 hours to kill any possible insect eggs, then repackage in heavy plastic bags, rigid plastic containers, or glass jars for longer storage. Pack tightly, but without crushing the tomatoes, and store containers in a cool, dry, dark place. For best flavour, use within one year.

Sun-drying Line racks or deep trays with double layers of muslin. Arrange the tomatoes cut side up, leaving room for air circulation. To protect from insects, cover with muslin or nylon netting, pulled taut to keep it off the tomatoes, and secured with tape. Let dry in the hot sun, above the ground. If using trays that have no air holes, turn tomatoes after juice

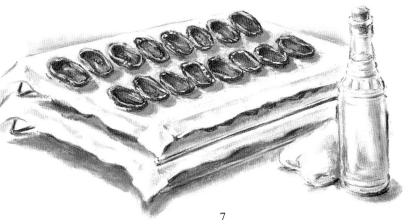

has evaporated from the cavity, then daily for 2–4 days, or until all the moisture has evaporated. During cool nights or rain, bring the racks indoors and check frequently for moulding. If mould forms, wipe it away with a clean cloth moistened with white vinegar or a solution of 1 tablespoon household liquid bleach to 2 pints water.

Oven drying Cover the bottom shelf of the oven with foil or a baking tray, to catch any drips. Preheat the oven to 80°C/175°F, or lower if your oven offers this option (foods dry best between 54°C–66°C/130°F–150°F). Place the prepared tomatoes cut side up on drying trays. Place the trays in the oven, leaving air space between them. Prop open the oven door at least 10cm/4in to help the tomatoes dry (you don't want them to cook). Place a small fan outside the oven to circulate the oven air, periodically changing the fan's position. When using a convection-oven, preheat to 60°C–65°C/140°F–150°F. Proceed as for conventional ovens, except leave the door ajar only about 1cm/½in. The fan is built in.

Let the tomatoes dry for 6–16 hours, reducing heat toward the end of the drying period. Turn trays frequently to prevent scorching and remove individual pieces as they are done.

Food-dehydrator drying Arrange the tomatoes, about 5cm/2in apart, cut-side up on the trays. Dry them on high for 10–16 hours or according to the manufacturer's instructions.

Using Dried Tomatoes

Sun-dried tomatoes are a unique ingredient with their own special flavour. Perfect for pasta sauces, pizzas or salads, sun-dried tomatoes have particular affinities for certain kinds of ingredients: garlic, Mediterranean herbs and vegetables, olives, olive oil, seafood and poultry.

Dried Tomatoes Refresh in boiling water for 2–10 minutes, then drain and use. Or you can make fabulous preserves using the recipes in Chapter 2. (If you plan to preserve the tomatoes soon after drying, you will not need to refresh them first.) If the tomatoes are not dried properly, they will disintegrate in the jar; you may have to experiment to get the texture right. The quality of sun-dried tomatoes varies by brand and sometimes they may taste tough and salty. If this happens, refresh the tomatoes in a few changes of boiling water until the texture and flavour improve.

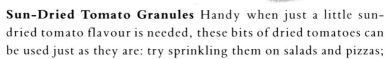

Sun-Dried Tomato Granules Handy when just a little sun-dried tomato flavour is needed, these bits of dried tomatoes can be used just as they are: try sprinkling them on salads and pizzas; or adding them to stir-frys, soups, or stews. For softer texture, refresh them with boiling water. You can make your own by finely chopping the loose, dried variety.

10

Sun-Dried Tomatoes Packed in Oil These are ready to use straight from the jar, either with or without their oil. When you use the oil along with the tomatoes, be sure to replenish the jar with fresh oil to keep the remaining tomatoes covered and to prevent moulding. When the tomatoes are gone, you can use the delicious tomato-flavoured oil that remains; it's wonderful in salad dressings or for sautéeing fresh vegetables. Once opened, preserved tomatoes must be stored in the refrigerator.

Sun-Dried Tomato Paste Consisting of sun-dried tomatoes, olive oil, garlic, herbs and seasonings, the paste is great for adding flavour to sauces or pasta dishes. To make your own, simply place some of your sun-dried tomatoes packed in oil in a food processor with some of the olive oil and whirl until blended to a paste. Keep the paste in a sealed jar in the refrigerator, where it will keep for several months.

11

PRESERVES

Sun-Dried Tomatoes with Herbs

225g/8oz sun-dried tomatoes	2 cloves garlic, cut into slivers
2 sprigs rosemary	2 tsp mixed peppercorns
2 sprigs thyme	4 juniper berries
2 bay leaves	600ml/1 pt light olive oil

*P*lace the sun-dried tomatoes in a bowl, cover with boiling water, and let stand for 10 minutes. Drain well on kitchen paper, then divide evenly among the jars with all the remaining ingredients except the oil. Shake the jars well to mix. Pour in the oil and seal. Leave in the refrigerator for 2 weeks before using. Store for up to 6 months. *Makes about 900ml/1½pt (enough for 3 × 300ml/½ pt jars).*

NOTE Keep a constant supply of these tomatoes on hand — they can be used for just about everything. Try them whole in sandwiches, or finely chopped and sprinkled over salads or into cooked pasta. Or, for sun-dried tomato paste, let stand for 2 weeks, remove the juniper berries and bay leaves and purée in a food processor.

12

Sun-Dried Tomatoes with Baby Mozzarella & Basil

75g/3oz sun-dried tomatoes
4–5 sprigs basil
225g/8oz fresh baby mozzarella
   cheese

6 black peppercorns
600ml/1 pt extra-virgin olive oil

*P*lace the sun-dried tomatoes in a bowl, cover with boiling water, and let stand for 10 minutes. Drain well on kitchen paper. Place a few sun-dried tomatoes in each of the jars, then add a few basil leaves and a few baby mozzarella. Continue layering in this way until the first 3 ingredients are used. Add 2 peppercorns to each, then pour in the oil. Seal and leave in the refrigerator for at least 1 week before using. Store for up to 1 month.

Makes 900ml/1½ pt (enough for 3 × 300ml/½ pt jars).

Olives & Sun-Dried Tomatoes

50g/2oz sun-dried tomatoes
175g/6oz stoned black olives
100g/4oz stoned green olives
½ small lemon, thinly sliced, then cut into wedges
3 fresh jalapeño chillies
600ml/1 pt extra-virgin olive oil

*P*lace the sun-dried tomatoes in a bowl, cover with boiling water, and let stand for 10 minutes. Drain well on kitchen paper, then dice. Divide the sun-dried tomatoes among the jars, then add the remaining ingredients except the oil and shake the jars well to mix. Pour in the oil, seal and leave in the refrigerator for at least 1 week before using. Store for up to 6 months. *Makes 900ml/1½ pt (enough for 3 × 300ml/½ pt jars).*

Greek-Style Sun-Dried Tomatoes

75g/3oz sun-dried tomatoes
175g/6oz cubed feta cheese
3 tbsp coriander leaves
1 tbsp mustard seeds
600ml/1 pt virgin olive oil

*P*lace the sun-dried tomatoes in a bowl, cover with boiling water, and let stand for 10 minutes. Drain well on kitchen paper; then cut into thin strips. Divide the sun-dried tomatoes among the jars; then add the remaining ingredients. Shake the jars well to mix. Seal and leave in the refrigerator for at least 1 week before using. Store for up to 1 month. *Makes 900ml/1½ pt (enough for 3 × 300ml/½ pt jars).*

NOTE Use this preserve to make an original Greek salad. Fill a large, shallow salad bowl with 1 head of coarsely torn cos lettuce. Add green sweet pepper rings, thinly sliced red onion, kalamata olives and cucumber slices. Top with the sun-dried tomato mixture and drizzle with 3–4 spoonfuls of the marinating oil. Sprinkle with the juice of 1 lemon and serve.

Red Pesto

16 sun-dried tomatoes packed in oil, drained
4 cloves garlic
4 tbsp pine nuts
100g/4oz freshly grated Parmesan cheese
150ml/¼ pt olive oil
¼ tsp freshly ground black pepper

*P*lace the sun-dried tomatoes, garlic, pine nuts, Parmesan, 5 tablespoons of the olive oil and the pepper in a food processor or blender. Whirl until smooth. Transfer to an airtight container and add the remaining oil on the top. This pesto can be stored for 1 week in the refrigerator. *Makes about 750ml/1¼ pt.*

NOTE This is also a good spread for a sandwich of focaccia, grilled aubergine, smoky Gouda, basil leaves, grilled red pepper and Dijon mustard.

STARTERS & BREADS

Grilled Chèvre in Grape Leaves

24 sun-dried tomatoes packed in oil, drained
12 grape leaves, preserved in brine, rinsed and drained
2 logs chèvre cheese (about 100g/4oz each), cut into 6 slices each
1 loaf country bread, thickly sliced

*P*lace two sun-dried tomatoes, slightly overlapping, in the centre of one grape leaf. Top with 1 chèvre slice. Fold up to form a parcel and arrange on a plate seam side down. Continue making parcels in this way until all but the bread has been used. Place the parcels on a rack under the grill for about 5 minutes, turning once, until hot. Serve at once with the bread. *Serves 4.*

NOTE These parcels can also be cooked on the barbecue. Place them in a grilling basket to keep them from falling through the rack.

Clams in Sun-Dried Tomato Stock

1kg/2¼lb clams

2 tbsp sunflower oil

1 carrot, thinly sliced

2 shallots, minced

1 stalk celery, sliced

1 small leek, finely chopped

450ml/16fl oz dry white wine

¼ tsp each salt and freshly ground black pepper

2 tbsp sun-dried tomato paste

2 tbsp chopped fresh parsley

1 small baguette French bread, sliced

Scrub the clams under cold running water and discard any with cracked shells or any that are not firmly closed. Heat the oil in a large pan over medium heat, add the carrot, shallots, celery and leek, and sauté for about 5 minutes until softened. Pour in the wine and add the seasoning. Add the clams and stir to combine. Cover and cook for 5–10 minutes, shaking occasionally, until shells open (discard any that remain closed).

Strain the clam cooking liquid into another pan; cover the clams to keep them warm. Bring the stock to a gentle boil, then stir in the sun-dried tomato paste and parsley; remove from the heat. With a slotted spoon, transfer the clams to serving dishes. Pour the strained stock over the clams. Serve at once, with the French bread. *Serves 4.*

NOTE For a one-dish meal, try serving the clams and stock with cooked fresh pasta, such as tagliatelle or fettucine.

Tomato Galettes

225g/8oz frozen puff pastry dough, thawed
4 large Roma tomatoes, sliced
¼ tsp salt
1 egg, beaten
50g/2oz Parmesan cheese shavings
4 basil sprigs

Sauce

2 tbsp olive oil
4–5 shallots, finely chopped
2 cloves garlic, crushed or minced
4 large Roma tomatoes, peeled, seeded and diced
8 sun-dried tomatoes packed in oil, drained and diced
2 tbsp coarsely chopped basil
¼ tsp freshly ground black pepper

*P*reheat the oven to 220°C/425°F/Gas Mark 7. On a lightly floured surface, cut the pastry into quarters, then roll each piece into a 13cm/5in round. Prick lightly in the centre with a fork, place on baking trays, and refrigerate for 15 minutes.

Meanwhile, to make the sauce, heat the oil in a frying pan over low heat. Add the shallots and garlic and sauté for about 5 minutes until softened. Add the Roma tomatoes and sun-dried tomatoes and cook for 2–3 minutes more. Stir in the basil, season with pepper and cook gently for 5 minutes more.

Divide the sauce evenly among the four pastry rounds, leaving a 1cm/½in border. Arrange the sliced Roma tomatoes on top so that they overlap. Season each galette, then brush the border with the beaten egg (do not brush beyond the top edge or the dough will not rise). Bake for 12–14 minutes, or until the pastry is crisp. Sprinkle with the Parmesan and place a basil sprig on each galette before serving. *Serves 4*.

Marinated Vegetable Platter

1 small aubergine, quartered lengthways
2 small courgettes, halved lengthways
1 each red and yellow sweet peppers, quartered and seeded
8 asparagus tips
2 red onions, quartered
175ml/6fl oz extra-virgin olive oil
2 tbsp sun-dried tomato paste
1 shallot, minced
1 red chilli, seeded and diced
1 clove garlic, crushed or minced
2 tbsp fresh oregano leaves
1 tbsp red wine vinegar
¼ tsp each salt and freshly ground black pepper
225g/8oz Sun-Dried Tomatoes with Baby Mozzarella & Basil
(page 13), drained
175–225g/6–8oz torn rocket leaves

*B*rush the aubergine, courgettes, peppers, asparagus and onions with 1½ tablespoons of the oil and barbecue or grill for about 10 minutes, turning occasionally, until tender. Place in a glass or ceramic dish and let cool.

Combine the sun-dried tomato paste, shallot, chilli, garlic, oregano, remaining oil, vinegar

22

and seasoning in a bowl. Pour the mixture over the vegetables and stir to coat. Cover and marinate for at least 1 hour in a cool place.

Drain the vegetables, reserving the marinade, and set aside. Place the rocket in a bowl, pour some of the grilled vegetable marinade over the leaves, toss well, and divide among 4 plates. Arrange the vegetables on top of each. With a fork or slotted spoon, divide the Sun-Dried Tomatoes with Baby Mozzarella & Basil among the plates, on top of the vegetables. *Serves 4.*

Bacon, Courgette & Sun-Dried Tomato Muffins

225g/8oz plain flour

3 tsp baking powder

¼ tsp salt

*6 slices bacon, cooked, drained and
    crumbled*

*8 sun-dried tomatoes packed in oil,
    drained and diced*

1 courgette, coarsely grated

50g/2oz shredded Cheddar cheese

225ml/8fl oz milk

1 egg

*4 tbsp butter, melted and
    cooled*

Preheat the oven to 220°C/425°F/Gas Mark 7. Grease a 12-cup muffin pan (or use paper baking liners); set aside. Sift the flour, baking powder and salt into a bowl. Stir in the bacon, sun-dried tomatoes, courgette, and two-thirds of the cheese. Make a well in the centre. In another bowl, combine the milk, egg and butter, blending well. Pour the liquid into the flour well all at once and fold just until dry ingredients are moistened. The batter should be lumpy. Fill each prepared muffin cup two-thirds full with batter and sprinkle with the remaining cheese. Bake for 20–25 minutes, or until golden brown. Transfer to a wire rack to cool. *Makes 12.*

Sun-Dried Tomato & Ricotta Bread

275–350g/10–12oz bread flour
1½ tsp active dry yeast
2 tsp salt
8 sun-dried tomatoes packed in oil,
    drained and diced

2 tsp chopped fresh rosemary
175ml/6fl oz warm water (about
    50°C/120°F)
100g/4oz ricotta cheese
2 tbsp extra-virgin olive oil

*M*ix 275g/10oz of the flour, the yeast, half the salt, and the rosemary in a large bowl. Make a well in the centre, pour in the water, and add the ricotta, olive oil and sun-dried tomatoes; stir into the flour mixture until combined. Transfer to a lightly floured surface and knead for 10 minutes until the dough is springy and elastic, adding more flour as needed to prevent sticking. Place in a clean, lightly oiled bowl and cover. Let rise in a warm place for about 2 hours, until doubled in size.

Knead again lightly for 1–2 minutes until smooth. Shape into a ball and smooth down the top. Transfer to a greased baking tray. Cover and let rise for about 1 hour until doubled in size.

Preheat the oven to 220°C/425°F/Gas Mark 7. Dissolve the remaining salt in 1 tablespoon hot water. Cool. Score the top of the loaf diagonally with a sharp knife. Brush with the salt water. Bake for 10 minutes; reduce the temperature to 180°C/350°F/Gas Mark 4 and bake for 10–15 minutes more. To test, tap the bottom; it should sound hollow. Cool on a wire rack.

SALADS & SIDE DISHES

Marinated Baby Aubergines

12 baby aubergines, halved
    lengthways

3 tbsp olive oil

6 sun-dried tomatoes packed in oil,
    cut into strips

3 tbsp pine nuts

2 tbsp chopped fresh parsley

Marinade

Juice of 1 lemon

3 tbsp olive oil

2 tbsp white wine vinegar

2 tbsp sugar

¼ tsp each salt and freshly ground
    black pepper

*B*rush the aubergines with the oil and grill for about 10 minutes, turning once, until cooked through and golden. Transfer to a shallow dish.

To make the marinade, combine the lemon juice, oil, vinegar, sugar and seasoning. Pour the marinade over the warm aubergines, then sprinkle with the sun-dried tomatoes, pine nuts and parsley. Marinate for at least 1 hour or cover and refrigerate overnight (return to room temperature before serving). *Serves 4.*

NOTE The aubergines can also be cooked in a ridged cast-iron frying pan. Be sure to turn and rotate them to create an attractive criss-cross pattern.

Roasted Potatoes, Shallots & Sun-Dried Tomatoes

450g/1lb baby new potatoes
225g/8oz small shallots, peeled
3 tbsp extra-virgin olive oil
1 tbsp chopped fresh sage

2 tsp chopped fresh rosemary
¼ tsp coarse sea salt
6 sun-dried tomatoes packed in oil,
*   finely chopped*

*P*reheat the oven to 190°C/375°F/Gas Mark 5. Place the potatoes and shallots in an ovenproof dish; drizzle over 2 tablespoons of the oil and sprinkle with the sage, rosemary and salt. Bake for 45 minutes, stirring occasionally, until the potatoes and shallots are well browned. Transfer to a serving dish and stir in the sun-dried tomatoes and remaining olive oil. *Serves 4.*

NOTE The earthy flavours of this dish marry well with simple grilled or roasted meats and poultry.

Aubergine with Raisins & Honey

Sauce

1 tbsp butter

1 tbsp flour

300ml/½ pt milk

¼ tsp each salt and white pepper

3 tbsp olive oil

1 onion, chopped

900g/2lb aubergines, cubed

150g/5oz bulgur

1 tsp cumin seeds

2 tsp honey

Juice of 1 lemon

50g/2oz raisins

12 sun-dried tomatoes packed in
  oil, chopped

*T*o make the sauce, melt the butter in a small pan over low heat. Add the flour and cook, stirring, for 1 minute. Remove from the heat and gradually pour in the milk. Bring to the boil and continue cooking, stirring constantly, until the sauce thickens. Reduce the heat and simmer gently for 2–3 minutes more. Season with the salt and pepper.

Preheat the oven to 200°C/400°F/Gas Mark 6. Heat the oil in a large pan over medium heat. Add the onion and sauté until softened. Add the aubergine and cook gently for 5–10 minutes until tender. Stir in the bulgur, cumin seeds, honey, lemon juice, raisins and sun-dried tomatoes and cook for 10 minutes more. Transfer to an ovenproof dish and spoon the sauce on top. Bake for 25–30 minutes until golden and bubbling. *Serves 6.*

Ricotta-Stuffed Red Peppers

Sauce

1 red onion, chopped

1 tbsp olive oil

450g/1lb tomatoes, peeled, seeded and chopped

2 tbsp sun-dried tomato paste

120ml/4fl oz dry white wine

1 clove garlic, crushed or minced

¼ tsp each salt and freshly ground black pepper

2 red sweet peppers, halved, seeded and blanched

350g/12oz ricotta cheese

1 egg, beaten

6 sun-dried tomatoes packed in oil, drained and minced

3 tbsp torn fresh basil leaves

3 tbsp freshly grated Parmesan cheese

¼ tsp each salt and freshly ground black pepper

*P*reheat the oven to 180°C/350°F/Gas Mark 4. To make the sauce, sauté the onion in the oil until softened. Add the remaining ingredients and cook for about 15 minutes until thickened.

Meanwhile, mix the ricotta, egg, sun-dried tomatoes, half each of the basil and Parmesan, and the seasoning. Spoon into the peppers and arrange in an ovenproof dish. Top with the sauce, then the remaining Parmesan. Bake for 25–30 minutes. Garnish with the remaining basil. *Serves 4.*

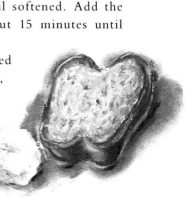

29

Mediterranean Summer Ragoût

2 aubergines, sliced crossways
1½ tsp salt and ½ tsp freshly ground black pepper
2 yellow sweet peppers
120ml/4fl oz olive oil
6 large mushrooms, thickly sliced
½ tsp each ground cumin and coriander
8 tomatoes, peeled, seeded and chopped
8 sun-dried tomatoes packed in oil, cut into strips
2 Spanish or other mild onions, thinly sliced
2 cooking apples, peeled, cored and chopped
120ml/4fl oz plain yoghurt

*T*o prepare the vegetables, place the aubergine in a colander, toss with 1 teaspoon of the salt, and set aside for at least 30 minutes. Rinse well, then pat dry with kitchen paper. Grill the peppers until their skins are blackened and charred. Let cool a little, then peel, seed and cut into quarters. Heat 2 tablespoons of the oil in a large frying pan over medium heat. Add the mushrooms, cumin and coriander, and sauté just until browned.

Spread half each of the tomatoes and sun-dried tomatoes in the bottom of an oven-proof casserole. Top with a layer of half each of the peppers, onion, apple and seasoning. Add the mushrooms, then continue layering with the remaining tomatoes, sun-dried tomatoes, peppers, onion, apple and seasoning.

Preheat the oven to 160°C/325°F/Gas Mark 3. Heat the remaining oil in a large frying pan, add the aubergine and sauté in batches until golden brown on both sides. Drain on kitchen paper, then arrange them over the vegetables in a slightly overlapping layer. Cover tightly with foil and bake for 1 hour until tender and cooked through. Serve hot with the yoghurt. *Serves 6.*

Golden Chicken Salad

Juice of 1 small lime
3 cloves garlic, crushed or minced
1 tbsp sun-dried tomato paste
½ tsp ground cumin
½ tsp each salt and freshly ground black pepper
120ml/4fl oz cup olive oil
4 chicken breasts, skinned, boned and diced
3 tbsp white wine vinegar
175g/6oz bulgur
3 tbsp snipped fresh chives
8 sun-dried tomatoes packed in oil, drained and cut into strips
1 head Webb lettuce, washed and leaves separated
8 mini pitta breads

Combine the lime juice, garlic, sun-dried tomato paste, cumin and half the seasoning. Stir in half the olive oil. Add the chicken and toss in the mixture to coat evenly. Cover and marinate for 30 minutes, or overnight in the refrigerator.

Spread the chicken pieces over a foil-lined grill pan and grill for about 10 minutes, turning occasionally, until cooked through and golden brown. Transfer to a bowl and stir in the remaining oil and the vinegar. Let cool.

Meanwhile, place the bulgur in a bowl and add enough boiling

32

water to cover. Let stand for 30 minutes until the grains are softened. Stir well and drain if any water remains. Strain the oil mixture from the chicken and stir the oil into the bulgur, with half the chives and the remaining seasoning.

Line a serving platter with the lettuce leaves. Spoon the bulgur on top. Arrange the sun-dried tomatoes and chicken on top and garnish with the remaining chives. Serve with the pitta bread. *Serves 4 as a main dish.*

Tricolour Salad

50g/2oz fresh mozzarella
    cheese, sliced
12 sun-dried tomatoes packed in
    oil, drained and chopped
2 small avocados, halved and
    peeled

5 tbsp extra-virgin olive oil
2 tbsp balsamic vinegar
¼ tsp each salt and freshly ground
    black pepper
12 basil leaves, thinly sliced

*D*ivide the mozzarella among 4 serving plates and arrange the sun-dried tomatoes on top. Slice each avocado half into a fan shape and arrange on top of the tomatoes.

In a small bowl, whisk the olive oil with the balsamic vinegar and seasoning. Drizzle over the salads and garnish each one with a sprinkling of the basil. *Serves 4.*

NOTE These ingredients also make a terrific sandwich. Drizzle the dressing over thick slices of any good Italian bread. Arrange the avocados, cheese and sun-dried tomatoes on top, then grill. Sprinkle with finely chopped basil.

Potato, Salami & Olive Salad

900g/2lb baby new potatoes
1 tsp salt
175g/6oz peeled and coarsely
    chopped salami
100g/4oz diced cooked ham
225g/8oz Olives & Sun-Dried
    Tomatoes (page 14), drained
5 tbsp plain yoghurt

1 tbsp chopped fresh parsley
1 loaf rye bread, sliced

Dressing

1 tbsp red wine vinegar
¼ tsp salt
1 tsp wholegrain mustard
4 tbsp light olive oil

*P*lace the potatoes in a pan of water with the salt and bring to the boil over high heat. Cook for 15–20 minutes until tender.

Meanwhile, to make the dressing, place the vinegar, salt and mustard in a small bowl. Whisk until blended, then gradually pour in the oil, whisking until thick.

When the potatoes are cooked, drain, then cool slightly before cutting into chunks. Place in a salad bowl and toss with the dressing. Add the salami, ham, Olives and Sun-Dried Tomatoes, and yoghurt. Mix gently. Sprinkle with the parsley and serve with the rye bread. *Serves 4 as a main dish.*

Spinach, Prosciutto & Bean Salad

225g/8oz cannellini (white beans), soaked overnight and drained
1¼ tsp salt and ¼ tsp freshly ground black pepper
1 loaf ciabatta or other Italian bread
6 tbsp olive oil
2 tbsp red wine vinegar
1 clove garlic, crushed or minced
1 tsp Dijon mustard
450g/1lb fresh baby spinach leaves, rinsed and patted dry
8 slices prosciutto, trimmed and cut into slivers
8 sun-dried tomatoes packed in oil, drained and thinly sliced
2 tbsp chopped fresh parsley

*P*lace the beans in a large saucepan and add cold water to cover. Bring to the boil, then lower the heat and cook for 30 minutes. Add 1 teaspoon of the salt and continue simmering for 30–40 minutes more, or until tender. Drain and let cool.

Preheat the oven to 180°C/350°F/Gas Mark 4. Wrap the bread in foil and place in the oven for 10 minutes to warm through.

Meanwhile, place the oil, vinegar, garlic, mustard and remaining seasoning in a screw-top jar and shake until the dressing is thoroughly combined.

Divide the spinach leaves among 4 serving plates. Top with the prosciutto and the beans. Arrange the sun-dried tomatoes on top and drizzle the dressing over each. Sprinkle with the parsley and serve with the warm bread. *Serves 4 as a main dish.*

NOTE When in season, rocket leaves can replace the baby spinach.

Four Tomato Salad

2 tbsp olive oil

1 tbsp balsamic or red wine vinegar

2 tsp wholegrain mustard

1 tsp honey

¼ tsp each salt and freshly ground black pepper

225g/8oz cherry tomatoes, halved

225g/8oz yellow tomatoes, halved or quartered

225g/8oz small Roma tomatoes, cut into wedges

16 sun-dried tomatoes packed in oil, drained

50g/2oz piece Parmesan cheese, shaved

6–8 tiny basil sprigs

*P*lace the oil, vinegar, mustard, honey and seasoning in a screw-top jar and shake until well combined. Place all the tomatoes in a salad bowl and pour in the dressing. Toss to coat, cover and set aside for at least 1 hour to allow the flavours to blend. Just before serving, toss the tomatoes with the Parmesan and garnish with the basil sprigs. *Serves 4.*

PASTA, PIZZA & POLENTA

Fusilli with Prawns & Avocado

400g/14oz dried pasta corkscrews
  (fusilli)
3 tbsp olive oil
275g/10oz cooked peeled prawns
8 sun-dried tomatoes packed in oil,
  cut into strips
1 large avocado, peeled, stoned and
  coarsely chopped

8 stoned black olives, quartered
2 tbsp balsamic vinegar
¼ tsp each salt and freshly ground
  black pepper
1 tbsp chopped fresh tarragon or
  basil

Cook the pasta in a pan of boiling salted water for 10–12 minutes, or until *al dente*. Rinse under cold running water and drain. Transfer into a salad bowl and toss with the olive oil. Add the prawns, tomatoes, avocado and olives and mix until blended. Gently stir in the balsamic vinegar and seasonings. Garnish the salad with the tarragon or basil and serve. *Serves 4.*

Warm Polenta Sandwiches

600ml/1 pt vegetable stock

100g/4oz quick-cooking polenta

3 tbsp olive oil

350g/12oz sliced mixed
   mushrooms, such as button,
   brown cap and shiitake

2 cloves garlic, crushed or minced

2 tbsp chopped fresh parsley

8 sun-dried tomatoes packed in oil,
   chopped

¼ tsp freshly ground black pepper

Salad

1 tbsp red wine vinegar

¼ tsp each salt and freshly ground
   black pepper

1 tsp sun-dried tomato paste

3 tbsp olive oil

275–350g/10–12oz mixed torn
   lettuce leaves, such as curly
   endive, radicchio and escarole

50g/2oz rocket, torn

*P*lace the stock in a pan and bring to the boil. Add the polenta
in a slow steady stream, stirring constantly to prevent any
lumps from forming. Reduce heat and simmer, stirring constantly,
for 5–10 minutes, until the polenta begins to come away from
the sides of the pan. Pour into a greased 20-cm/8-in square pan,
smooth the surface, and let cool for at least 30 minutes.

Preheat the oven to 190°C/375°F/Gas Mark 5. When the
polenta is cool, turn out and cut into 16 squares. Use half the oil
to brush each square on both sides and grill for about 5 minutes
on each side until golden. Set aside.

Heat the remaining oil in a frying pan over medium heat. Add the mushrooms, garlic and parsley and sauté for about 5 minutes until completely softened. Stir in the tomatoes and pepper and cook for 1 minute more. Set aside.

To make the salad, place the vinegar, seasoning and tomato paste in a salad bowl and whisk to blend. Gradually add the oil, whisking until thick. Add the lettuce leaves and rocket and toss to coat. Set aside.

Place half the polenta slices on a greased baking tray and distribute equal amounts of the mushroom mixture on top of each. Top with the remaining slices of polenta and bake for about 5 minutes, or until heated through. Arrange the polenta sandwiches on serving plates and place a serving of salad alongside each sandwich. Pour any pan juices over the salads and serve at once. *Serves 4.*

Courgette, Garlic & Sun-Dried Tomato Pasta

8 large cloves garlic

450g/1lb courgettes, thickly sliced

3 tbsp extra-virgin olive oil

400g/14oz dried pasta shells
(conchiglie)

4 tbsp sun-dried tomato paste

2 tbsp chopped fresh mint

¼ tsp each salt and freshly ground
black pepper

Few each parsley and mint sprigs

Preheat the oven to 200°C/400°F/Gas Mark 6. Blanch the garlic cloves in a pan of boiling water for 2 minutes; then drain, peel and pat dry with kitchen paper. Mix the courgettes and garlic with 1 tablespoon of the oil and place them in a small ovenproof dish. Bake for 15–20 minutes until the vegetables are golden and tender.

Meanwhile, cook the pasta in a pan of boiling salted water for 10–12 minutes, or until *al dente*. Drain, transfer to a serving bowl, and stir in the remaining oil and the sun-dried tomato paste. Stir in the courgettes and garlic with the pan juices, then add the chopped mint and seasoning. Garnish with the parsley and mint sprigs. *Serves 4.*

Pasta with Red Pesto & Spicy Sausage

450g/1lb small dried pasta shapes, such as orecchiette or cappelletti
450g/1lb spicy sausage, such as Italian or chorizo, sliced
1 tbsp olive oil
175ml/6fl oz Red Pesto (page 16)
1 tbsp torn fresh oregano leaves

Cook the pasta in plenty of boiling salted water for 10–12 minutes, or until *al dente*. Meanwhile, sauté the sausage in a nonstick frying pan for about 5 minutes until browned and cooked through. When the pasta is cooked, drain, and transfer to a serving dish. Stir in the oil, Red Pesto, and sausage. Sprinkle with the oregano and serve. *Serves 4.*

Chèvre & Prosciutto Pizza

Sauce

900g/2lb tomatoes

1½ tbsp olive oil

1 red onion, sliced

1 clove garlic, crushed or minced

8 sun-dried tomatoes packed in oil, coarsely chopped

1 tsp sugar

1 tbsp chopped fresh basil

¼ tsp each salt and freshly ground black pepper

2 ready-made pizza crusts, about 23cm/9in in diameter

2 tbsp olive oil

350g/12oz prosciutto slices, chopped

100g/4oz crumbled firm chèvre

100g/4oz stoned black olives

2 tbsp capers, drained

To make the sauce, score the bottoms of the tomatoes with an 'X', pour boiling water over to cover, and let stand for 1 minute. Drain and peel off the skins. Cut each tomato in half, then scoop out and discard the seeds. Chop the tomatoes coarsely and set aside. Heat the oil in a pan over low heat, add the onion and garlic, and cook for 5 minutes until softened. Add the tomatoes, sun-dried tomatoes, sugar and basil and simmer gently for 10 minutes. Season and set aside.

Preheat the oven to 220°C/425°F/Gas Mark 7. Place the pizza crusts on baking trays and brush lightly with the oil. Spread the tomato sauce over the crusts, just up to the edges. Sprinkle with the prosciutto, then top with the chèvre, olives and capers. Bake for 15–20 minutes until browned and serve at once. *Serves 4.*

Gnocchi Bolognese

2 tbsp olive oil

1 onion, chopped

1 carrot, chopped

175g/6oz sliced button mushrooms

50g/2oz chopped chicken livers

2 cloves garlic, crushed or minced

450g/1lb minced beef

400g/14oz peeled, seeded and
    chopped tomatoes

8 sun-dried tomatoes packed in oil,
    chopped

2 tbsp sun-dried tomato paste

120ml/4fl oz dry white wine

120ml/4fl oz beef stock

1 bay leaf

½ tsp each salt and freshly ground
    black pepper

2 tbsp chopped fresh parsley or
    basil

25g/1oz freshly grated Parmesan
    cheese

Gnocchi

450g/1lb russet potatoes, peeled

100g/4oz plain flour

8 sun-dried tomatoes packed in oil,
    minced

¼ tsp salt

*I*n a large frying pan, combine the oil, onion, carrot, mushrooms, chicken livers and garlic over medium-high heat. Cook, stirring, for about 2 minutes. Add the beef, increase the heat, and cook for 2 minutes more. Add the tomatoes, sundried tomatoes and paste, wine, stock, bay leaf and seasoning. Bring to the boil, reduce the heat, cover and simmer for about 30 minutes.

Meanwhile, to make the gnocchi, cook the potatoes in boiling, salted water until tender but not mushy. Drain thoroughly, then press through a sieve. Sieve the flour into a large bowl and make a well in the centre. Add the potatoes, sun-dried tomatoes and salt. Using your hands, gradually knead the flour into the potato mixture until a dough is formed. Transfer to a floured surface. Shape the dough into long rolls about 2.5cm/1in in diameter, then cut into 2cm/¾in pieces.

Bring a large pot of salted water to the boil. Gently drop the gnocchi into the water and poach for 2–3 minutes until they rise to the surface. With a slotted spoon, transfer the gnocchi to serving dishes and top with the sauce. Sprinkle with the parsley or basil and serve with the Parmesan. *Serves 4.*

MEAT & POULTRY

Poussin Creole

Creole seasoning

2 tsp garlic salt

1 tsp dried oregano

1 tsp ground cumin

½ tsp each cayenne, hot red pepper flakes, and dried thyme

Juice of 2 limes

2 tsp coarsely ground black pepper

8 sun-dried tomatoes packed in oil, finely chopped

5 tbsp olive oil

4 poussins or junior free-range chickens (about 675g/1½lb each), split

675g/1½lb large baking potatoes, cut into thick wedges

*T*o make the seasoning, combine all the herbs and spices in a small bowl and stir to blend. Combine the lime juice, pepper, sun-dried tomatoes, 1 teaspoon of the Creole seasoning and 3 tablespoons of the olive oil in a shallow, ovenproof glass or ceramic dish. Add the poussins and baste with the oil mixture. Cover and marinate in the refrigerator overnight.

Preheat the oven to 200°C/400°F/Gas Mark 6. Toss the potato

wedges in 1½ tablespoons of the Creole seasoning and the remaining oil. Arrange on a baking tray and bake for 35–40 minutes until golden brown and cooked through.

Meanwhile, grill or barbecue the poussins, basting with the lime mixture as they cook. Allow about 15 minutes on each side. Test with a skewer; the poussins are done when the juices run clear. Serve with the potatoes. *Serves 4.*

NOTE The Creole seasoning can be used like ordinary salt and pepper, whenever a zippy flavour is desired: sprinkle it on chops, burgers, or even jumbo prawns before barbecuing.

Honey-Mustard Glazed Duck

4 boneless duckling breast halves

2 tsp salt

3 tbsp sun-dried tomato paste

1 tsp Dijon mustard

1 tbsp honey

1 tsp chopped fresh rosemary

450g/1lb mixed vegetables, such as
   baby carrots, baby squash and
   mange tout, steamed

*P*reheat the oven to 180°C/350°F/Gas Mark 4. Prick the skin side of the duck all over and rub with salt. Place the meat, skin side up, on a rack in a roasting tin. Bake for 15 minutes.

Meanwhile, combine the sun-dried tomato paste, mustard, honey and rosemary until blended. Brush over the meat and bake for 15 minutes more, or until just cooked through. Remove from the oven and let rest for 5 minutes before cutting into slices. Serve at once, with the steamed vegetables. *Serves 4.*

Chicken & Sun-Dried Tomato Risotto

1.15l/2 pt chicken stock
6 tbsp butter
1 onion, finely chopped
2 boneless, skinless chicken breast
    halves
350g/12oz arborio rice

½ tsp each salt and freshly ground
    black pepper
16 sun-dried tomatoes packed in
    oil, cut into strips
4 tbsp freshly grated Parmesan
    cheese
3 tbsp chopped fresh parsley

*B*ring the stock to the boil in a large pan, then reduce the heat and keep it at a gentle simmer. Melt half the butter in a large heavy-bottomed pan over medium heat. Add the onion and sauté until softened. Add the chicken and cook until just browned. Add the rice and stir with a fork for 2–3 minutes, until the grains are well coated with butter. Add a ladleful of the hot stock and cook, stirring frequently, until all the stock is absorbed. Continue adding stock one ladleful at a time, stirring constantly, waiting until each addition is absorbed before adding the next. Season after about 10 minutes.

When the risotto is thick and creamy (about 20–25 minutes) begin tasting. The rice is done when it is *al dente*. Just before serving, stir in the remaining butter and the sun-dried tomatoes, Parmesan and parsley. Serve at once. *Serves 4.*

Turkey & Bacon Kebabs

12 slices bacon

225g/8oz boneless turkey, cubed

24 sun-dried tomatoes packed in
oil, cut in half

275–350g/10–12oz torn mixed
lettuce leaves, tossed with
dressing

450g/1lb basmati rice, cooked

Sauce

120ml/4fl oz plain yoghurt

2 tsp prepared horseradish

1 tbsp wholegrain mustard

1 tsp honey

¼ tsp each salt and freshly ground
black pepper

Cut each slice of bacon crossways into four pieces. Wrap
and stretch each piece of bacon around a cube of turkey
and half a sun-dried tomato, and thread onto eight wooden
skewers. Place the kebabs on a grill rack and grill for about 10
minutes, turning once, until the bacon is crisp and the meat is
cooked through.

Meanwhile, to make the sauce,
combine the yoghurt, horseradish,
mustard, honey and seasoning
in a small bowl and stir until
blended. Serve with the
turkey kebabs, salad and
rice. *Serves 4.*

Peppered Beef

900g/2lb beef tenderloin
60ml/2oz sun-dried tomato paste
2 cloves garlic, crushed or minced
1 tbsp crushed mixed peppercorns
3 tbsp wholegrain mustard
1 tbsp honey
¼ tsp salt
675g/1½lb broccoli, steamed
900g/2lb baby new potatoes, steamed

*P*reheat the oven to 180°C/350°F/Gas Mark 4. Trim excess fat from the beef, then tie with string at 2.5-cm/1-in intervals. In a bowl, combine the sun-dried tomato paste, garlic, peppercorns, mustard, honey and seasoning and stir until blended. Spread the mixture over the beef to cover it completely.

Place the beef on a rack in a roasting tin and roast for 50 minutes–1 hour for rare, 1 hour 10 minutes for medium, and 1 hour 10 minutes–1 hour 20 minutes for well-done. Let stand for 10 minutes before removing the string and carving into thick slices. Serve with the broccoli and new potatoes. *Serves 4–6.*

NOTE This sun-dried tomato and pepper coating is equally delicious on roast leg of lamb.

Baked Chicken with Spinach & Sun-Dried Tomatoes

Sauce

1½ tbsp olive oil

1 onion, chopped

2 cloves garlic, crushed or minced

675g/1½lb tomatoes peeled, seeded and chopped

8 sun-dried tomatoes packed in oil, chopped

Few sprigs thyme, leaves stripped

1 tbsp chopped fresh parsley

¼ tsp each salt and freshly ground black pepper

1½ tbsp olive oil

4 boneless, skinless chicken breasts

½ tsp each salt and freshly ground black pepper

225g/8oz fresh spinach, stemmed

75g/3oz mozzarella cheese, thinly sliced

450g/1lb long-grain rice, cooked

*T*o make the sun-dried tomato sauce, heat the oil in a deep frying pan over low heat. Add the onion and garlic and sauté gently until softened. Stir in the tomatoes, sun-dried tomatoes, herbs and the seasoning. Cover and simmer gently for about 20 minutes. Let cool, then process in a food processor.

Preheat the oven to 180°C/350°F/Gas Mark 4. Heat the oil in a large ovenproof casserole. Season the chicken breasts with half the seasoning, place in the casserole and cook until golden brown on both sides. Spoon the sun-dried tomato sauce on top.

Steam the spinach for 1–2 minutes, then drain well. Arrange over the tomato sauce, sprinkle with the remaining seasoning and top with the slices of mozzarella. Bake for 25–30 minutes, or until the chicken is cooked through and the mozzarella is bubbling. Serve hot with the rice alongside. *Serves 4.*

Chilli Cornbread Pie

175g/6oz black beans, soaked
   overnight and drained
1½ tsp salt and ½ tsp freshly
   ground black pepper
1 tbsp olive oil
1 onion, chopped
2–3 green chillies, seeded and
   minced
450g/1lb boneless shoulder or leg
   of lamb, cubed
450g/1lb tomatoes, peeled, seeded
   and chopped
3 tbsp sun-dried tomato paste
2 tsp chilli powder

3 tbsp chopped fresh coriander
275–350g/10–12oz torn mixed
   lettuce leaves, tossed with
   vinaigrette

Topping

225g/8oz yellow cornmeal
3 tbsp plain flour
6 minced sun-dried tomatoes
1 tsp salt
1 tbsp baking powder
2 eggs, beaten
175ml/6fl oz milk
3 tbsp light olive oil

*P*ut the beans in a large pan with cold water to cover by 5cm/ 2in. Bring to the boil and cook for 30 minutes. Add 1 teaspoon of the salt and continue cooking for about 1 hour more, or until the beans are tender. Drain.

Preheat the oven to 200°C/400°F/Gas Mark 6. Heat the oil in a large pan. Add the onion and chillies and sauté over low heat for 5 minutes until softened. Add the lamb and cook until browned. Stir in the tomatoes, beans, tomato paste, chilli powder, coriander and remaining seasoning. Bring to the boil, cover, and simmer for 10–15 minutes.

Meanwhile, to make the cornbread topping, combine the cornmeal, flour, minced sun-dried tomatoes, salt and baking powder. Stir in the eggs, milk and oil and mix until well combined.

Transfer the meat mixture to an ovenproof dish and top with the cornbread mixture. Bake for 35–45 minutes until golden brown and firm to the touch. Serve hot with the salad alongside. *Serves 4–6.*

FISH & SEAFOOD

Salmon en Papillote

250g/9oz French Puy lentils
1¼ tsp salt and ¼ tsp freshly ground black pepper
2 baby leeks, green and white part, thinly sliced
4 salmon fillets (about 150g/5oz each), skinned and boned
24 sun-dried tomatoes packed in oil, finely chopped
3 tbsp chopped fresh dill
4 tbsp butter
75ml/3fl oz dry white wine

Put the lentils in a large saucepan with 1.4l/2½ pt of cold water and bring to the boil. Add 1 teaspoon of the salt, reduce heat and simmer gently for about 30 minutes, or until tender.

Meanwhile, preheat the oven to 200°C/400°F/Gas Mark 6. Cut out 4 circles of parchment paper, 13 inches in diameter. Crease each circle down the middle and place a bed of leeks on one side, leaving a 1-cm/½-in border, then lay the salmon fillets on top. Divide the sun-dried tomatoes among the 4 parcels, then sprinkle each with the dill and remaining seasoning.

Melt the butter in a small pan, then stir in the wine. Pour the liquid over the salmon fillets. To make the parcels, gather up the edges of the paper folding them together little by little, tucking the final corner under to seal. Place on a baking tray and bake for about 15 minutes, or until cooked through.

Drain the lentils and divide among 4 plates. Serve the salmon alongside, either unwrapped or still in its parcel. *Serves 4.*

Seafood with Fennel & Tomatoes

3 tbsp olive oil

1 large onion, chopped

1 small fennel bulb, sliced

2 cloves garlic, crushed or minced

4 large tomatoes, peeled, seeded and chopped

8 sun-dried tomatoes packed in oil, cut into strips

1 bouquet garni (1 sprig each parsley and thyme plus 1 bay leaf)

1 tsp grated lemon rind

¼ tsp ground saffron

150ml/5fl oz dry white wine

175g/6oz monkfish fillet, cubed

100g/4oz red snapper fillet, cubed

100g/4oz clams, well scrubbed

225g/8oz jumbo prawns, uncooked, peeled and deveined

¼ tsp each salt and freshly ground black pepper

2 tbsp snipped fresh chives

450g/1lb fresh tagliatelle, cooked and tossed with olive oil

Put the oil in a wok or large frying pan, add the onions, fennel and garlic and sauté over medium heat for about 5 minutes, or until softened but not coloured. Add the tomatoes, sun-dried tomatoes, bouquet garni, lemon rind, saffron and wine. Bring to the boil, then simmer gently for 15 minutes.

Add the monkfish and simmer for 5 minutes, then add the red snapper, clams and prawns, and simmer for 5 minutes more until just cooked through. Discard any clams that remain closed. Season, sprinkle with the chives and serve with the tagliatelle. *Serves 4.*

Rolled Sole with Red Pesto

8 small sole or other flat fish fillets
(about 900g/2lb total)
3 tbsp Red Pesto (page 16)
3 tbsp lemon juice
120ml/4fl oz fish or vegetable
stock

¼ tsp each salt and freshly ground
black pepper
100g/4oz each leeks, asparagus
and carrots, cut into 5-cm/2-in
pieces
100g/4oz each mange tout and
baby corn cobs, trimmed

C ut each fillet along the natural centre line into two pieces.
In a small saucepan, combine the pesto, lemon juice, stock
and seasoning. Roll up the fish fillets loosely and put in the pan.
Bring to the boil, then reduce the heat, cover and simmer gently
for about 10 minutes, or until the fish is just cooked through.

Meanwhile, steam the vegetables. Spoon them onto plates,
top with the fish, and drizzle with the pan
juices. *Serves 4.*

Trout Stuffed with Scented Rice

4 tbsp butter

3 cloves garlic, crushed or minced

175g/6oz sliced button mushrooms

350g/12oz long-grain white rice

600ml/1 pt vegetable stock

8 sun-dried tomatoes packed in oil,
    cut into strips

Juice and rind of 1 lemon

4 tbsp chopped fresh tarragon

4 whole trout (about 175–225g/
    6–8oz each), cleaned and boned

½ tsp each salt and freshly ground
    black pepper

Preheat the oven to 200°C/400°F/Gas Mark 6. Melt the butter in a pan, then add the garlic and mushrooms and sauté gently for 2–3 minutes. Stir in the rice and cook for 2–3 minutes more, stirring, until the rice is coated in butter. Stir in the stock and bring to the boil. Reduce the heat, cover and simmer gently for 15–20 minutes, or until all the stock has been absorbed and the rice is tender. Remove from the heat and stir in the sun-dried tomatoes, lemon juice and rind and tarragon.

Divide the rice mixture among the trout, stuffing it into the cavity of each. Place the trout in a buttered ovenproof dish, spoon the remaining rice around the trout and season. Cover with buttered foil and bake for 20–25 minutes, or until the trout are cooked through. *Serves 4.*

Index